Somebody Ought to Testify!

Stories to uplift and encourage your Faith

By:

GLORIA FOWLER

Palmetto Publishing Group
Charleston, SC

Somebody Ought to Testify!

I have tried to recreate events, locales and conversations from my memories of them. In order to maintain their anonymity in some instances I have changed the names of individuals and places, I may have changed some identifying characteristics and details such as physical properties, occupations and places of residence.

First Edition

Printed in the United States

ISBN-13: 978-1-64111-290-1
ISBN-10: 1-64111-290-5

DEDICATION

This book is dedicated to my grandchildren who encouraged me, my mother who inspired me and my husband who walked this road with me. May this book be passed from generation to generation to testify how GREAT God was to our family!

INTRODUCTION

Jeremiah 29: 11 - 12 "For I know the plans that I have for you," declares the LORD, plans to prosper you and not to harm you, plans to give you hope and a future. Then you will call on me and come and pray to me, and I will listen to you. You will seek me, and find me when you seek me with all your heart."

In this modern world people are asking why don't we see more miracles. The answer is simple we don't believe. The saying "seeing is believing" fits. As human beings we tend to believe only what we see, not what we can't see; but that is not what Faith is. Faith is believing in things we can't see. That's why when heavenly events happen they need to be shared with other people to help build their faith. Faith comes from hearing the word, but also by testifying to the result of that faith. When people hear what God has done to other people they think if He can do it for them, then He can do it for me. When that faith is built up then God can do GREAT wonders!

The following events are precious to my family…not that we are anything special. We just believed and had faith along with a lot of friends and churches that prayed for us.

We are grateful for everything the Lord has done for us. Every day he blesses us in one way or another. It could be a big miracle, a small blessing or just his watching over us. His gifts come in all sizes.

I hope that after reading this book, that you too will believe and receive your miracle and God's visitation in your life; and when you do , testify to what God has done for you so other people can hear and believe. Then they too can testify and it goes on and on. Think of what great things God can do if everyone would just believe and share!

I Chronicles 16:8 "Give thanks unto the LORD, call upon his name, make known his deeds among the people."

Matthew 17:20 "And Jesus said unto them, because of your unbelief: for verily I say unto you, If ye have faith as a grain of mustard see, ye shall say unto this mountain, Remove hence to yonder place; and it shall remove; and nothing shall be impossible unto you."

Proverbs 3:5 "Trust in the LORD with all your heart and do not lean on your own understanding; In all your ways acknowledge Him, And He shall direct your paths.

Revelations 12:11 "And they overcame him by the blood of the Lamb, and by the word of their testimony; and they loved not their lives unto the death".

Psalms 103:2 "Let all that I am praise the Lord; may I never forget the good things he does for me."

Psalms 9:1 "I will give thanks to you, LORD with all my heart; I will tell of all your wonderful deeds."

If God tells us in his word to testify, then why don't we!

CONTENTS

1.

WHY ME LORD?

I began putting this book together after two of my grandsons suggested it. I had recently retired from thirty-four years of teaching and I was sitting at my computer feeling a little depressed. I was missing my students and my classroom. Jonathan and D.J. both came to talk to me at separate times and suggested that I share my stories with other people by writing a book. As a teacher I had an opportunity to share my stories with over a thousand children. My classroom was my pulpit. I would have devotions and share a story with the children everyday about how good God is and now I was no longer teaching.

After thinking about it for a while I decided maybe this would be a good idea. I could write a book for my grandchildren and when they had children they could read it to them. This would be a keepsake- a memory book-of Nanny and Pappa and their faith in God. So I began to write and as I wrote I began to realize just how blessed we were. After several weeks of writing I began hearing a still small voice saying, "Somebody's Got to Testify". After hearing that voice for several days, I asked the Lord: "OK, God what do you want me to do?" I didn't get an answer. Several more weeks passed and while I'm still writing, God is still saying "Somebody's Got to Testify". Then one night God woke me up and said, "Go to speak at Cym's church". I said Lord you want me to do what?" I heard again "Go speak at Cym's church". (Cym is my middle daughter) . I went back to sleep and the next morning I asked God to show me if this was really him speaking to me. It was Sunday morning and my daughter, Cym called me. This was unusual because we both are so busy getting ready for church that we don't have time to call. I decided to put feelers out to see if it really was God speaking to me, so I asked Cym to talk to her pastor's wife and see if she would let me come speak to her ladies group about a book I am writing. She said she would. Later that afternoon she called me back and said that the pastor didn't want me to just talk to the ladies, but he wanted me to speak on a Wednesday night. Then she said, "Mom you won't believe what the pastor preached about this morning". He preached about "Somebody Has to Testify". I thought "OK, Lord, I'm getting nervous now". I have no problem teaching to large groups of kids (60 - 100 at a time); but adults. What if they get bored and don't like my stories. Lord these are precious personal things that happen to my family. Now I began to back peddle....maybe it wasn't the Lord talking to me, maybe I misunderstood the voice. Panic set in. So I stopped thinking about it. The next day we had to travel to Kings Bay, Georgia and on the way back I again began talking to God in my head and find excuses why I couldn't do what God was asking me. I tried to distract myself from thinking and turned the radio on and would you believe the song on the radio was "Somebody's Got to Testify". "OK, Lord, I finally got the message in this hard head". I know what you want me to do. So I went to this church and shared three of my testimonies. Believe it or not I didn't pass out and the church seemed to enjoy my stories, but more importantly I wanted them to be uplifted and blessed. I wanted them to realize how good God is.

I can't travel all over the world to testify of God's goodness, but I can send my book in my place. I hope if you read these stories they will bless you as much as they blessed me when I kept remembering them.

Somebody's Got to testify
and that person is
Me!

2.

A FLYING CAR

In 1965, my dad came to know the Lord in a very personal way and was called to the ministry. After several months he decided to go to College to learn what he needed to about being a pastor. So we moved to Cleveland, Tennessee to attend College. My parents became very busy going to school, working jobs, and starting a youth choir at the church we attended. We also traveled as a family singing at different churches. We worked hard for a couple of years, then my dad was offered a pastorate in Ogden, Utah. He was very excited at the thought of having his own congregation. One afternoon dad called a family meeting and we gathered at our meeting place which was my parents bed and we began to talk about what we should do. My mom and dad shared their feelings about the move and listened to our concerns, but in the end my dad decided this was the right move.

It's a long way to Utah and we had a lot to do to get ready. The next several weeks were filled with packing and getting things ready for that big move. We put everything we had into the largest U haul trailer we could find that was safe enough for our car to pull. Bright and early one Sunday morning we set out on our great adventure, little did we know what kind of an adventure it would be.

It was a bright and sunny day when we left Cleveland. The mountains were beautiful . On one side we looked at the high mountains and the other side of the road were deep valleys. We almost couldn't see the bottom. Our car was running great pulling the trailer. At least we thought so. About halfway through the mountains the car started jumping and swaying a little bit. Then all of a sudden the car was being jerked from one side of the road to the other. My dad could barely hold it on the road. My brother, sisters and I were in the back seat being tossed around like rag dolls. Finally, my dad said, "kids start praying I can't hold the car on the road. I'm going to put my foot on the brake, but I don't know what will happen. We will either hit the mountain or drop into the raven." Dropping into the raven would mean the trailer would land on top of the car and would probably kill us instantly.

Dad had no choice he had to do something, so he waited a second and then put his foot on the break. The car jerked and we did a couple of figure eights in the road and the last thing we remember was dropping into the raven. A little while later confused and in shock we realized we were ok. We looked around to see where we were at and realized that we were on the other side of the mountain about a mile from where we had gone into the ravine. We were turned facing the opposite direction. We were amazed when we saw where we were at and where God took us. The car and trailer were both in perfect condition. As we began thinking about what had just happened we were amazed and thankful, because we knew it was only by the grace of God that we survived. The mighty hand of God picked up our car and trailer and carried us out of harms way. After we sat for a few minutes we thought about what just happened. My mom said she remembered heavy traffic passing us, but when dad decided to slam on breaks there were no other cars on the road. Isn't it wonderful to know that God prepared the road for our accident so no one else could be hurt. Needless to say we learned two valuable lessons on that trip. First, DON"T move on Sunday! Second, Make sure you double check with God that you are going where He wants you to be.

God has His children in the palm of his hand where He protects them. He sometimes asks us to go to places just to see if we are willing. Not necessarily that He really wants us to go, just that we would be willing to. That day God found out that we were willing to go wherever He wanted to send us.

Just like in God's word Abraham was told by God to take his son and sacrifice him, but God didn't really want him to be sacrificed He just wanted to know how much Abraham loved Him. God sent a lamb to be the sacrifice, instead of Isaac and God blessed Abraham for his obedience. If we are obedient to God nothing is impossible for Him.

Jeremiah 32:27 "Behold, I am the Lord, the God of all flesh is there anything to hard for me?"

And on that day we knew the answer to that question. NOTHING is too hard for our God.

3.

SALTY POTATO

My husband and I met in 1972 while attending a Bible College. It was a whirlwind romance. Love at first sight. Our first date was on February 13, 1972 and were married June 30, 1972. We had a very hard time trying to go to school and work. Money was scarce. We had only been married a few months when we really found out how hard life could be.

It was three days until payday and all we had left in the cupboard was one potato. So that potato was our lunch and what we were going to do for dinner God only knew. So I began baking that potato and all the time we were praying for God's help.

I finished baking the potato. My husband trying to be helpful divided it in half , put butter on it and salted it. The problem was he salted that potato too much and I couldn't eat it. He felt bad, but enjoyed the whole potato. I left him to his potato and decided to check the mail. All the way to the mailbox I was praying for the Lord to help us. I opened the box and began to look at the mail. Bills, bills and then an envelope from one of my parents friends appeared. It had been mailed in June and finally found us in September. The envelope contained a congratulations card on our marriage and also a $10.00 bill. I looked at the envelope again and it had the right address on it, but it took over three months to find us. Accident, don't think so. God knew we would need that money on that day. His timing is always right. Now some people may think ,oh ten dollars that's not much money; but in 1972 we could buy at least three bags of groceries. In reality, we only used eight dollars because we used two dollars to fill up our tank with gas (gasoline was 17 cents a gallon and we had a VW bug). We bought enough groceries to last us over a week. Not only did He supply the need for the day, He sent more. God is so good!

Matthew 6:26 "Behold the fowls of the air; for they sow not, neither do they reap, nor gather into barns; yet your heavenly Father feedeth them; Are ye not much better than they"

Philippians 4:19 "But my God shall supply all your need according to his riches in glory by Christ Jesus."

4.

PRAYER MEETING

While attending the Bible College in Tennessee I witnessed one of God's wondrous miracles. On Wednesday nights the students at the college would have services in Brown Auditorium. Several young ministers rotated preaching and would be in charge of the services. One particular service the Spirit of God was moving so strong that the students decided to have a prayer line. (this is where students line up on two sides and people who need special prayer walk through the line. The people on each side lay their hands on your back and pray a special prayer for you).

Students started coming to the front of the auditorium and form a line for prayer. One particular student walked to the stage. She was wearing an elevator shoe, because one of her legs was shorter than the other. She had been accustomed to the fact that her legs would never be the same. That's what the doctors said; but her faith made her go forward. She went into the line and walked down as each student prayed for her. At the end of the line there was a lot of excitement. She was sitting on the floor and she began taking off her shoe. Standing up she began shouting. As she was walking you could tell that both of her legs were now the same size. What man couldn't do, God did! God had healed her in the prayer line. Her faith was a testimony of what God can do!

It only takes the faith of the grain of a mustard seed to move a mountain. How much does it take to stretch a leg? Nothing is to hard for my God!

Matthew 19:26 " But Jesus beheld them, and said unto them, with men this is impossible; but with God all things are possible."

5.

A DEAD GARDEN

In 1976, My husband and I went to a pastorate in a very small city in South Carolina. The church was small only about 15 people attended. Most of those were older people in poor health and needed a lot of attention from the pastor. It was very difficult for David to hold down a job because the people always needed him at the hospital. Needless to say my husband didn't keep jobs very long. It was a struggle to pay bills and keep food on the table. We knew that God would take care of us, but as human beings we tend to worry. There was a garden in our back yard that had once supplied a former pastor with food; but that was many years ago. We walked through the garden and looked at it hoping some glimmer of a sprout could be seen. We saw nothing, it was dry, and dead. Nothing could grow in that garden. It was past restoring. We were really praying for God to supply our need. We hadn't paid attention to the garden for a couple of days, but one morning we opened the door and looked at the garden. We almost passed out with what we saw. That dead garden had begun to grow beautiful vegetables almost overnight. God heard our prayer! Not in months or weeks, but in days we had corn, tomatoes, peppers, cucumbers and squash. We began to pick the vegetables and the more we picked the faster they were all growing. We picked enough to eat, fill our freezer, gave some to other people who needed them and even sold some. That money helped us get milk and bread for our babies. After a couple of weeks, almost overnight the garden was dead again. You couldn't even tell that it had just produced anything. This was a miracle from God who supplied food for His children. If I hadn't seen it with my own eyes, I would not have believed it could have happened; but, it did. I saw it and I ate from it! And oh, how my faith grew!

Psalms 37:25 " I have been young, and now am old; yet have I not seen the righteous forsaken, nor His seed begging bread."

Philippians 4:19 "But my God shall supply all of your needs according to His riches in glory by Christ Jesus."

If you're a child of God, he's not going to let you go hungry. If He will feed the birds how much more will he take care of and feed his children. If you have the faith as the grain of mustard seed, God said we could move mountains. It only takes a little faith!

6.

PARTY TIME

In 2003, a precious saint of God, my Mother -in-law was called home. Her name was Grace. We were greatly saddened by her passing, especially my husband. He was a late in life baby and was closer to his mom than the other children. We stayed a few days after the funeral and then we decided to go home. At that time we lived in Charleston, SC and would have to travel about four hours to reach our home. We were tired, but felt like we needed to go home.

That night began the strangest week we had ever experienced. I woke up in the middle of the night hearing people in my room laughing and talking. It was as if there were several groups at different places in the room talking and laughing. I couldn't understand their words, but you could tell they were having a good time. They were joyful about something that was happening; you could feel it. I looked outside to see if the people next door were having a party. No, all was quiet. I checked all the TV sets to see if someone had left one on. The sounds were in no other room except our bedroom. The voices didn't scare me. I felt peace and such a comforting spirit. I wanted to just sit there and listen all night in hopes I could understand what they were saying. But I didn't, I turned over and went to sleep. The next night it happened again. This time there seem to be more people in the room. They were still laughing and talking and this continued happening for the next 4 days. Finally, on Friday night I woke up and just sat listening. I looked over at my husband who was now sitting up listening also and said to him, "please tell me I'm not going crazy and that you hear a party in our room". He said he heard it and had been waking up all week listening to the party. As we were talking about the sounds and listening we realized that God was giving us a miracle. The Lord drew back the curtain of Heaven and allowed us to hear the joy of a Christian going home. He was sending comfort to us over our loss by letting us hear the party that was going on in Heaven. The Bible says that we will rejoice with the angels in heaven over a child of God coming home; and that's what we heard the Angels, family and friends rejoicing over Grace's home coming.

After that week we were still sad because we missed her, but happy because she was in God's heaven and He was giving her a welcome home party.

Psalms 116:15 "Precious in the eyes of the Lord is the death of His saints."

It's hard to loose a loved one; but if they are Christians at least you have the joy of knowing they will be with Jesus and one day you will see them again.

7.

I KNOW THERE IS A HEAVEN

In 1982, my father- in -law, L.J. was diagnosed with Parkinson disease. For fifteen years he suffered with this disease. By the end of 1997 he was in the last stages. We had a hospital bed put into his living room so he could be close to his family and be a part of what was going on. He did not want to die in a hospital. L.J. had been a minister for over 40 years and it was hard to watch how this disease was affecting him. He was unable to walk and could barely talk. We could tell it would not be long before we would loose him.

During the third week of October LJ slipped into a coma. For three days he was completely out, but looked so peaceful. One morning all of a sudden he woke up. We could barely hear what he was saying, but he was calling all of his children to come to the bed he had something to say. As they all gathered round he began to speak in a quiet, but excited voice he said, "Its real, Its real. Heaven is real. I have been there and I know its real". A few minutes later he went back into a coma and the next week, on Halloween night he went home to be with the Lord.

God allowed my father-in-law to catch a glimpse of Heaven and come back to share with us that heaven is real. **Heaven is real** and one day all those who love Him will see Him. One day we will get to see what my father-in-law saw. Heaven!

I Corinthians 2:9 "But as it is written, eye hath not seen, nor ear heard, neither have entered into the heart of man, the things which God hath prepared for them that love Him."

8.

SCARED OF THE DARK

My husband joined the military in 1975. His desire was to be a Chaplain, but he ended up going into another field. This job put him being gone a lot. We would never know where he was going or how long he would be gone. This presented a problem for me. We had only been married a couple of years when our home had been broken into, because of this I had developed the fear of staying by myself during the night. When David would leave I would booby trap my house. I put chairs under each door knob and placed bottles under each window. (I know I'm not the only wife that ever did this) Even after all of this I was still afraid and could not sleep at night. I would work all day and stay up all night. My work was suffering and I was exhausted. During one of his deployments, I put all of my girls in the same bed with me. (after I booby trapped the house) I still couldn't sleep. I paced the floor back and forth and finally took a knee (which I should have done earlier) and prayed for the Lord to protect us and let me get some sleep. I held my head up and looked at the doorway and there I saw an Angel. He had his armor on with his sword. His body filled the doorway so nothing could get through. I looked at his face and it was as if he was telling me go to sleep everything is going to be fine. I felt a sense of peace. I got up off my knees and went to bed. I went to sleep almost immediately. I slept all the way through that night. Since that time I have not been afraid to be alone at night because I know that God sent His Angel to watch over me.

Isn't It wonderful that God cares enough about His children that He sends Angels to protect us, and watch over us.

Psalms 91:11 "For he shall give his angels charge over thee, to keep thee in all thy ways."

Exodus 23:20 "Behold, I send an Angel before thee, to keep thee in the way, and to bring thee into the place which I have prepared."

9.

VISITING ANGELS

In 1983, the military sent our family to Germany. It is a beautiful country, but it was a very dangerous place at that time; because of the terrorist the military was put on alert. It was not unusual to see terrorist throwing rocks and tomatoes at anyone wearing a uniform. Bombs were put under the cars of Americans and sometimes they threw pipe bombs into the neighborhoods where Americans were living. We kept a packed suitcase under our bed in case we had to be evacuated quickly. Our daughters rode a bus to school that was guarded by soldiers. Their school was also guarded. We had to travel in groups because it was just too dangerous to travel alone. One time we had a white suitcase thrown in our complex by a moving car. The bomb squad came and checked it out, but it was only a dud. Dud or not that scared the wives that were in the subdivision. Needless to say it was nerve racking.

Our church held services in an old building in downtown Kaiserslautern. On Sundays we held services at 4:00 p.m. Our church building was in the middle of town and it had two entrances. One in the front at the street and one in the back. It opened into an alley. We had two guards at the front door and two at the back. They made sure they knew who came and who went out. We also had a light at the back of the church that lit up when anyone jiggled the back door. We thought we were pretty safe.

On this particular Sunday we were having a special play and everyone was excited. We arrived a little late. We past door inspection and quickly got into the sanctuary. As we were going in, we noticed two elderly American women sitting toward the back of the church. They stuck out like sore thumbs, mainly because of the way they were dressed. It was unusual to see elderly American women, especially traveling alone. We wanted to stop and welcome them, but we were late and had to get the play started. Promising to ourselves that we would get to them as soon as the play was over.

The play went off great and everyone was blessed by it. As soon as it was over we went to where the ladies had been, but they were not there. We went to the front door and asked if the two elderly American ladies had left. The guards said they did not see them go out the front door. So we went to the back door and again the guards said no elderly ladies left by way of the back door. In fact both guards said they didn't even come into the church by their doors. Now there are only two entrances and guards at both entrances said they did not leave by way of them, then where did they go? After talking it over with other people at the church we came to the only conclusion. We had just entertained Angels unaware.

We know this to be true for several reasons: (1) Guards were the only ones who could let people in or out of the doors. The guards said they did not let any elderly American ladies in or out of the back door or the front door. (2) It is very rare to see elderly American women, especially alone in

Germany. Elderly American women dress differently than elderly German women so its easier to tell the difference.

That night we were blessed to be visited by Angels. How Wonderful!

Hebrews 13:2 "Be not forgetful to entertain strangers; for there by some have entertained angels unaware.

10.

TOO MANY CHILDREN

My mother-in-law told me the story of how my husband almost didn't make it into this world. In 1952 doctors were scarce in small towns so most women who were pregnant would see a midwife. When Grace started seeing her, she began to give her medicine on each visit. Grace thought they were vitamins, but after a couple of visits she found out that they weren't. Grace already had three children so the midwife thought she did not need another baby. So she had been giving her medicine to miscarry her child. When she found out what had happened she started calling all the people of the church to pray that she would not miscarry. The Lord heard the prayers of the people in that small church and David, my husband was born.

What God intends to happen will happen no matter how people try to interfere with His plan. David was blessed in his mother's womb to become a disciple for him.

Isaiah 14:27 "For the LORD of hosts hath purposed, and who shall disannul it" and his hand is stretched out, and who shall turn it back?"

Jeremiah 29: 11 "For I know the plans I have for you, declares the Lord, plans for welfare and not for evil, to give you a future and a hope"

Proverbs 16:9 "The heart of man plans his way, but the Lord establishes his steps."

Proverbs 19:21 "Many are the plans in the mind of a man, but it is the purpose of the LORD that will stand."

Jeremiah 1:5 "Before I formed you in the womb I knew you, and before you were born I consecrated you; I appointed you a prophet to the nations."

David was called to preach when we was 17 years old and has been preaching God's word for over 50 years. Satan tried to take his life, but God said he is my called one. God is in control!

Psalms 139:13-14 "For thou hast possessed my reins; thou hast covered me in my mother's womb. I will praise thee; for I am fearfully and wonderfully made: marvelous are thy works; and that my soul knoweth right well.

11.

MY LITTLE GRACE

In 1976, I was diagnosed with a disease called Stein Leventhal Syndrome or otherwise known as Polycystic Ovarian Disease (PODS). I was told after having my second child that because of PODS I could not have anymore children. My husband loves children and was a little sad because he had always wanted us to have eight. I would always tease him and say that I would have the first two then he could have the rest. So we settled in to the fact that we would be a family of four. We did discuss the idea of later on adopting; but God's plans are not always our plans.

A few months later I started getting sick in the mornings and just feeling tired all the time. I had already had two children so I knew the symptoms of pregnancy, but I just threw it out of my mind because of what I was told by the doctors. It kept going on and one day I told my husband, If I didn't know any better I would say that I was pregnant. He suggested I go to the doctor just to make sure something else wasn't wrong. So I made an appointment with a gynecologist. He took lab tests and examined me and said no I was not pregnant. My problem was that I needed to get out more and work off my frustrations. My iron count was a little low so he prescribed vitamins and exercise. A week later past and another and I continued having symptoms. I was getting really upset because I thought maybe I was going crazy. So my husband decided to take me to another doctor where he did lab tests. The next day the doctors office called him at work and said congratulations your pregnant. When David told me I was stunned. I made an appointment with another doctor and went to have an examination. At the end he said I was defiantly pregnant, in fact he said your about five months pregnant. Now it was hard for me to understand how the first doctor who did the examination could not know that I was pregnant. It had only been a couple of weeks since I had seen him. I knew I was pregnant, but I was really happy that I wasn't going crazy!

The next couple of months went by and everything seem to be fine. In the middle of my seventh month my placenta ruptured and I was loosing the fluid that was protecting my baby. I was rushed to the hospital and examined and confirmed that almost all of my fluid in my placenta had drained out. I started running a temperature which was dangerous for me and also the baby.

The doctor came and told us that the temperature meant that there was a sign of infection which put both of our lives in danger. He told us if my temperature kept rising he would have to make the decision to take the baby. We knew that the baby would not be old enough to survive. I could feel the baby moving and after everything we went through I was determined they were not going to take my baby.

That night after my temperature had went up again the doctor came in and said he would give me till morning and if my temperature had not gone down the decision would no longer be mine. He would have to take the baby in order for me to live. I was scared.

My husband began calling parents and everyone he knew to help us pray that the temperature would go down and I could keep the baby. My mom and Dad got on an airplane to be with us no matter which way it went. We prayed all night and nothing changed. I felt like God was with us and we were in his hands. I finally fell asleep. The nurse woke me up about six and told me that my temperature had gone down. Praise the Lord. Prayer works!

The doctor came in and said that we were not out of danger. He said I could continue carrying the baby to full term, but either she would be born dead or deformed. There was also a chance I would not survive. I told him we were in God's hands and we will take our chances. He directed me to stay in bed for the rest of my pregnancy to keep what little bit of water was left inside. For the next two months I went into labor 11 times. In the latter part of the eighth month I expected them to go ahead and let me have the baby. But that was not to be. I literally carried her for 10 months. Finally my husband said enough is enough. He wanted this baby born in South Carolina not Texas. So over every ones disapproval and warnings we packed up to go to my in-laws house in Marion, South Carolina.

On the way to South Carolina we went through Atlanta and of course I started in labor. I asked David to stop and let me walk around a little bit and after a few minutes the contractions stopped. When we finally got to Marion the first thing I did was see a doctor. His name was Doctor Woo... He examined me and said that I had already dilated two centimeters and if I didn't have the baby this weekend he would induce me on Monday. So we managed to get through the weekend and on Monday morning he started the drip to induce labor. The contractions started and continued getting worse. At 7:00 p.m. our precious daughter was born. She was born what is called sunny side up. Meaning that her eyes were open looking to heaven when she came out. She was not born dead or deformed as the doctors said she would be. She was a perfectly healthy 8lbs 6 oz. baby girl. We named her Grace. She was given that name for two reasons: (1). My mom and my husbands mom both were named Grace. (2). It was only by the grace of God that she was born.

After she was born my husband and I thought about taking Grace to the first doctor who was a one star Surgeon General and introducing my "frustrations" to him.

This story only goes to show you that God is in control of our lives. What he wants to happen will happen. In His time and in His way. If we had listened to doctors and not to God, we would not have our precious Grace now.

Romans 8:28 "And we know that for those who love God all things work together for good, for those who are called according to His purpose."

Proverbs 19:21 "Many are the plans in the mind of a man, but it is the purpose of the Lord that will stand."

Job 12:10 "In his hand is the life of every living thing and the breath of all mankind."

12.

CANCER SCARE

While in Germany during a routine examination I was diagnosed with ovarian cancer. The dreaded "cancer word". The mention of that word can cause fear in anyone's heart, but I knew God would take care of me; Either on this earth or in Heaven. I was directed by my doctors to come back in a couple of weeks and we would discuss the next action. One of the first things I did was to call both sets of parents and asked for their prayers. Its wonderful to have parents that are prayer warriors. I also asked for prayer from my church there in Germany. Most all of them were so supportive and began praying for my healing, but then there were the few that asked me what sin had I committed. They said that the Lord would heal me of cancer If I would repent of whatever sin I had committed. That God was punishing me for those sins. I was shocked! I know they meant well, but I knew that any sin I had committed was under the blood when I got saved many years ago.

The next two weeks went by with a lot of prayer and hope that everything would be alright. I went back to the doctors office and after another examination and going over reports he told us that he could not find the cancer. I no longer had cancer! God answered another prayer for us.

Jeremiah 33:3 "Call unto me and I will answer thee and show thee great and mighty things which thou knowest not".

St. John 9:3 says "Neither this man nor his parents sinned,' said Jesus, " but this happened so that the works of God might be displayed in him."

Philippians 4:6 "Do not be anxious about anything, but in everything by prayer and supplication with thanksgiving let your requests be made known to God."

13.

THE NAILED WINDOW

In 1986, we were living on Maxwell Air Force Base in Montgomery, Alabama. Two of our three daughters were teenagers at this time and just like any other family with teenagers there comes a time of rebellion. Teenagers think they are to old to follow rules and think they know better than their parents. Our oldest daughter was that way. At 15 she thought she was grown and that her mom and dad did not understand her. I think its harder for the parents to go through this time period than it is for the teenager. We know exactly what they are going through because we have been there, done that and even bought the T-shirt to remind us of it.

One night about midnight the Lord woke me up and said that my daughter was climbing out of the window. Of course, half asleep I said, Lord you know she wouldn't do that. Then I laid back down to sleep. A few minutes later in a much firmer voice I heard him say, Your daughter is climbing out of her bedroom window. Needless to say I got up really fast that time because God meant business. I went into her room and sure enough she had climbed out of her window. I was shocked and scared about her being out so late at night by herself. I went to wake up my husband and told him that Steffaney had climbed out of her window. He looked at me and said, "No, she wouldn't do that." Just what I told the Lord. So I told him a second time and this time he jumped out of bed and went into her room and saw the window was open.

We both went outside to see if we could see her walking around, but it was so dark we couldn't see anything. I went to the road and looked around and saw nothing. I began to pray while I was standing in the road. "Lord please help me find my daughter", I turned around to the dormitories that were across the street and the Lord told me that's where she is. My husband went to the second floor and there she was with a bunch of friends. Her dad said get home and she did. When he arrived back home her window was nailed shut and we put her on restriction for eternity!

The moral to this story is not how bad or good my daughter was because she was a normal teenager. The thing I want you to notice is that God was watching out for my daughter. He took care of her even though she was making the wrong choice. She could have gotten hurt, but he woke us up and told us where she was. God is so good; He even looks after rebellious teenagers.

I Peter 5: 7 "Casting all your care upon him; for he careth for you".

14.

A RIDE IN THE PADDY WAGON

While in Germany, my husband got the opportunity to travel around and preach in different places. On one occasion we were invited to go to Frankfurt to preach at the local church. The service was scheduled on a Saturday night so we would not miss our church services. We had two other families that went with us. One family rode in our van and the other family followed in their van. The trip took a good two hours and we got to the church just in time for services to begin. Bob, who was following us told David that he didn't have enough gas to make it home so he was going to go get gas before the stations closed and would be back soon. The services started and David preached a good message, but by the end of the service Bob still had not returned. We waited a little longer and then his wife said, "we'll just go ahead and go home, maybe he got lost and decided just to go home." So all of us got into one VW van and started home. We ended up with 13 people in a seven passenger van. Talk about crowded. We were about an hour away from home going up an incline when the van lost power. We rolled onto the shoulder of the road to see what we could do. By this time it was getting really dark. The men decided they would walk the half mile to use the phone on the interstate to call for help. By the time they had walked back to the van the Polizi (police) were pulling up. The polizi spoke in broken English, but we tried to understand what he was saying. He had told my husband that he would call a taxi. My husband tried to explain that we needed more than one taxi. He kept saying "nine, nine" (no, no); until he shined his flashlight into the van and all of the children popped up from the floor. He busted out laughing and kept saying "yah, yah" (yes, yes). A few minutes later a vehicle known as the 'paddy wagon' showed up. This was a van like truck with no windows except for the drivers window and passenger side.

All thirteen of us piled into this paddy wagon and we started on our way. Now if you have ever been to Germany you know that you can't get off the interstate and then get back on. You have to travel a couple of miles ahead and then circle back to return to where you were. So we started taking dark, back roads in the woods. I looked at my friend sitting next to me and she looked terrified. I pictured in my mind tomorrows newspaper headline: "Thirteen bodies found in the woods". As if they could read my mind the two policemen started laughing. We drove a good 30 minutes before all of a sudden we were back on the interstate at a large diner. We all got out and went in. We thought the police were going to leave, but they just stayed watching over us. While the men were on the phone trying to get some help, we settled the children down and got them something to drink. A little while later they came into the diner and said they could not get in touch with anyone. So we sat down to try and figure out what to do. No sooner had we sat down then in walks the pastor of our church. He said he had also been preaching somewhere and decided to stop and get a drink. He said normally he never stops, but something told him to stop. We know that something was God! We explained that our van broke down on the road, so the preacher took the men home to pick up another vehicle to come back to get us. Funny thing happened when they got to where the van was. Bob drove up right behind them. Said he had gotten lost trying to find a gas station. They all got back in their vehicles and came to pick us up. When we were all safely in Bob's van ready to leave we noticed that the German police also left. They stayed to make sure we were safe. We all got home safely. The next day the men went to tow our van home and later we found out that our gear shaft had broken.

God synchronized all of the comings and goings of four families so that we would all be where we needed to be to help each other out. As a child of God you don't have to worry, he will always take care of you and send you help when you need it.

Philippians 4:19 "But my God shall supply all your need according to his riches in glory by Christ Jesus."

Romans 8:28 "And we know that for those who love God all things work together for good, for those who are called according to his purpose."

Isaiah 41:10 "Fear not, for I am with you; be not dismayed, for I am your God; I will strengthen you, I will help you, I will uphold you with my righteous right hand."

15.

A VALENTINE STORY

Growing up in a Pastor's family was very lonely. Most of the churches that we had were small churches and usually didn't have many teenagers. Which meant when we were old enough to date there were no Christian boys to date. My dads rule was we could only date Christian boys. That meant my sisters and I didn't date. Needless to say that kept us on our knees praying for the Lord to send us young people; and as we grew older that the Lord would send us the right companion. I put a little P.S. on my prayers and I told God I didn't want to marry a preacher! Never tell God what you are not going to do, because you will usually end up doing it!

When I graduated from High School my parents decided to send me to Lee University in Cleveland, Tennessee. I was excited with the idea of going to a college with a lot of young people that believed spiritually the way that I did. I started school in January and lucked out that my roommate was a girl that attended one of our former churches. (lucked out or God's plan). God knows what he is doing even if we don't. My roommate had already been to Lee for a year so she knew a lot of people. She introduced me to some of her special friends and there was one young man , his name was David ,that I found interesting. He had eyes elsewhere though. One night at chapel David asked my roommate if she wanted to go with him to church off campus. He was preaching that night. She said no, but then leaned back and pointed to me and said; she would. He looked at me and said "she can go if she wants too. Tell her to meet me outside". I looked at my roommate and said, "boy that was rude". But I started thinking, this could be my chance for him to notice me. So I got up and walked out the door and there he was waiting for me. (he said later on that something told him to wait).

There was another young lady with us who was coming to play the piano for him. So I got in the back seat of his VW bug and we drove to a small church out in the country. David did preach and I was very impressed with him. After church we drove back to the campus. As I was getting out of the car David asked if I wanted to walk a couple of blocks into town to a Café for apple pie. I said yes. Along the walk we talked, and talked and talked. I think we covered every topic we knew and the more we talked the more positive I was that this was the guy for me. We finally walked back to the dormitories and he said goodnight. No kissing, no holding hands, nothing. He just said good night and walked away. When he left I didn't know if he liked me or if I would ever see him again. That night was the day before Valentine Day. It was three days later before I saw him again. He came looking for me. He wanted to talk to me about something.

We went into the social room and sat down. He started out saying, "I know you won't believe me, but you have totally rocked my world." He went on to say that a girl he had been wanting to date called him on Valentines day and asked if he would go out with her. He said no that he had fallen for someone else. He said "in one night I have fallen in love with you and I know that God has sent you to me. I have thought of no one else but you for the last three days". And that began our whirlwind romance. The next week he asked me to marry him, but of course we had to wait till school was out. And we did. We had our first date on February 13th and got married on June 30th.

God had a plan for my life and even though it was hard for me to understand at the time, it all worked out. I didn't want to marry a preacher, but I did and couldn't have been happier about the idea. We had a lot in common: Both of our parents were pastors, both of our mothers played the piano and his mother's name is Grace Evelyn and my mother's name is Evelyn Grace. Isn't that strange.

When you put your life in God's hands he will guide you where you need to be, and who you need to be with. We have been married for 45 years and what God puts together stays together.

Jeremiah 29:11 "For I know the plans I have for you, "declares the Lord, "plans to prosper you and not to harm you, plans to give you hope and a future.

16.

ASK AND IT SHALL BE GIVEN

Thirteen years ago we came to pastor a small Native American church on the Natchez Kusso reservation in South Carolina. The church was a small white block building. Inside the stage was in a bad spot; in order to go to the restroom you had to walk over the stage. That means while the preacher is preaching the kids are going back and forth to the bathroom. This was very distracting for everyone. The pews were cracked and if you sat in the right spot you would get pinched. The carpet was old red carpet that was full of holes. People would trip when they walked on it. The place was a mess, but we loved it.

We saw the need to fix up God's house even though we had no money to do it. So David asked the people to band together and start praying for the Lord to send us some help. And He did!! For the next six months everything we asked for or even hinted we wanted appeared. We needed a pulpit, sound system, overhead projector, glass door and a file cabinet. Once we said we needed these things God gave them to us. One day a pastor two hours away said he had a shed they were cleaning out if we wanted to come up and see if there was anything we needed. When we got there we not only got a pulpit, but we had three. There were sound systems, microphones, glass doors, two overhead projectors, a file cabinet and a lot of others things that we were thankful for. Before the men left the pastor of the other church said he felt led to give us a check for $1,000. That money helped us buy new carpet and turn our stage around. A Baptist church was getting rid of very nice white pews and they gave them to us. They also had chandeliers they were getting rid of and sold them to us for hardly nothing. When we got the pews, we had to get rid of the old ones and we found out another small church needed pews so we gave them the old ones. They were very happy to get them. We also gave them one of the pulpits. So as we were receiving, we were giving to others who needed them.

One day as David was walking through a large church not far from us he notice a Remembrance table and two altar benches, which we needed, underneath a stack of furniture. He asked the pastor what was he going to do with the table and benches and he told David if he needed them he could have them. He was so excited he couldn't get them in the car fast enough. Now this was on Wednesday morning and by Wednesday afternoon we were heading to the church with our treasures. We wanted to surprise the church, so we got to the church early and placed the table and the altars at the front of the church. They looked so pretty sitting there. A little later the people started coming in. They came into the door and just stood there looking. Some began to cry. They were so overwhelmed with what God had given us they didn't know how to respond. The next morning David had to run out to the church. When he got there he heard music blaring and thought they had decided to have church without him. He unlocked the door and walked in and all of the ladies had their buckets of water and cleaning materials and were scrubbing the upholstery on the altars and cleaning the

Remembrance table. They said they had never had anything so beautiful.

We were so thankful for all that God had given us, but He didn't stop there. A few months later a Pentecostal church in the next city sent us enough money for a new roof, and A Catholic church sent us enough money to buy puppets for our children's ministry.

We never asked these churches for anything. They gave because God told them there was a need. When we pray with faith believing God will do great things for you. God did great things for us during this time. Not only by sending the things we needed, but also by showing our church what prayer and faith can do. We all learned a valuable lesson about prayer and faith. God never forgets about his children. What a mighty God we serve!

Hebrews 11:6 "And without faith it is impossible to please him, for whoever would draw near to God must believe that he exists and that he rewards those who seek him."

Proverbs 16:3 "Commit your work to the LORD, and your plans will be established."

Matthew 6:33 "But seek first the kingdom of God and his righteousness, and all these things will be added to you."

Jeremiah 33:3 "Call unto me and I will answer thee and show thee great and mighty things which thou knowest not."

17.

WE TOOK THE WRONG PATH

I believe that there are two things that keep God from doing what he wants to do, our disbelief and our interference; or rather our idea that we know better than God. That is what happened to us, we chose the wrong path and had to pay the price.

In 1979 it came close to the time that David was to reenlist in the Air Force. We had been away from home for almost four years and really wanted to go home or close to home. We decided to leave the Air Force and go back to school to finish our degrees. The emphasis being on the word we. We had prayed about it and convinced ourselves that this was what God wanted us to do. So when the time came we packed our things and moved back to Cleveland, Tennessee in the hopes of finishing our education.

We arrived in Cleveland three days later and found an efficiency hotel room to stay in until we could find a place to live. David went to find a job and after several days found a position at Bendix Corporation. After living in a hotel for a month, we finally found a house. As we began to get settled in we started working in a local church and thought things were finally looking up for us. The problem is when you walk off of God's path and get on your own path things will never be better. After working with Bendix for several months the company went on strike. The employees were paid $50 a week to walk the picket line. David tried to find another job, but no one wanted to hire someone that was on union strike. After a couple of months of the strike we had decided that we needed to make other choices so we could take care of our children. We called David's uncle who owned an upholstery shop in Anderson, South Carolina. His uncle was more than willing to give David a job and even offered to bring a truck and help us move. The next day Uncle Ralph and his son Todd came and moved us to Anderson. Thank the Lord for a caring family. When we got to Anderson David began working for his uncle. We rented a house owned by his parents and for the time being we were at least receiving a paycheck. About a month after we moved to Anderson our oldest daughter got scarlet fever.

When we thought we had crossed that hurdle all three of our daughters got the chicken pox and that followed with all three of them having the flu at the same time. We were exhausted and discouraged. We knew we were not where we were suppose to be. We were out of God's will and we knew it. So we really started praying for the Lord to put us back where we needed to be. We talked about it and David said he knew God wanted him back into the Military. So he went down to talk to a recruiter who said the service was not taking any former enlistees into active duty. David asked the Lord to show him if this was what he wanted us to do by opening the door for us to go back in. He called several recruiters but each one told him no, finally he called Charlotte, North Carolina recruiter and he said "how fast can you get here". Within 24 hours from that time we were back into the military, and we both sighed a sense of relief because we knew we had done the right thing. The one thing we were worried about was being stationed so far away from where we were at; but God solved that problem he sent us only two hours away, to Sumter, South Carolina. We got to the base and they told us it would be a couple of months to get into base housing, but God opened doors and within three days we had a house. It felt so good to finally have things working out for us, but it was only because we were back in the will of God. I know God allowed us to get out of His will so that we would see what it would be like without him. We found out and never want to go through that again. God takes care of his children even if it means allowing them to stray off his path. God said that He has a plan for us; a plan to uplift us and to have a better future. When we decided that we knew better than God we missed out of two years worth of His benefits. We learned the hard way to make sure that you check and double check what your next step is and make sure it's the one He wants you to take.

Proverbs 3:5 "Trust God with all of your heart and lean not unto your own understanding and in all ways acknowledge him and he shall direct your path."

I Corinthians 10:13 "No temptation has overtaken you that is not common to man. God is faithful, and he will not let you be tempted beyond your ability, but with the temptation he will also provide the way of escape, that you may be able to endure it."

18.

MOM

My mom was diagnosed with A Plastic Anemia which was caused by Gold shots given to her for rheumatoid arthritis. According to Dr. Graham, her oncologist, she was the only survivor of A Plastic Anemia (Read full story in her book "He was there All the Time"). She went through a lot for two years, but God was always with her. One story I want to share was when we took mom to The National Insitute of Health to get her spleen out. As we went into her room there was a bulletin board on her wall in front of her bed. There was a card pinned to it. We kept looking at it for several days and mom said someone before her must have left it. After a few days mom finally said for my sister to get that card and bring it to her. She got the card and turned a little white in her face. The card read 'I wish for you to have good health' and it was signed your loving mother Goldie. Funny thing my grandmother's name is Goldie, but she has been dead for over 50 years. She looked at the handwriting and said that it looked like her mother's handwriting. The nurse told her to take it home and said Your mother just wanted you to know that she was watching over you.

Mom had a spleenectomy and everything went fine. We were worried because of her bleeding situation that she would have problems, but she didn't. So after a couple of weeks she went home. When she got home one of the first things she did was check out the signature on the card with her mothers handwriting. And would you believe it looked exactly alike. God works in mysterious ways His wonders to perform.

That card encouraged my mom and the Lord knew that. We believe that God put that card in that room especially for my mom. God has been faithful to her during her illness, and her healing. When man did all they could do God came in and showed them what He could do!

According to The National Institute of Health they didn't do anything to help my mom. They told her it was God that touched her. Nice to know there are some Christian doctors with Faith. My mom is now 86 and still loves the Lord.

St. John 11:4 "When Jesus heard that he said, This sickness is not unto death, but for the glory of God, that the Son of God might be glorified thereby."

19.

DON'T CHASE THE BURGLAR

We were living in Charlotte, North Carolina when we were robbed. We were awakened one night with a burglar at the foot of our bed trying to get my television. I woke up and saw him at the foot of my bed. I shook David and said "there is a man in our room". About that time the man ran out of the room and for some strange reason I got up to chase him. The Lord only knows what I would have done if I had caught him, but I wasn't thinking about that at the time. Thank God I didn't catch him, he got out the kitchen window before I could get there.

We looked around and found out that they had taken a radio and some money, but that was not what we were worried about. Our daughters crib was also in the room. They could have taken her or even killed all of us in our sleep. We know that God had his hedge of protection around us so that no harm could be done to us. He also protects dumb women who jump up and try to catch a thief with nothing in her hand.

Psalms 91:11 "For He shall give His angels charge over thee, to keep thee in all thy ways.

20.

CANDY CAN BE DANGEROUS

We had gone for an interview with a small church in South Carolina. The church ran about 30. The people were very nice. The morning service was good and we stayed over to preach for the night service.

That night David was preaching and really into his message. There was a lady that had a three year old little girl. For some odd reason she allowed her little girl to run around the church while the preacher was preaching. This was a great distraction for the preacher as well as the people who were trying to listen. The little girl ended up on the side of the stage with David. All of a sudden her mother who was sitting in the auditorium started screaming, "shes dying, someone help her". The little girl was standing by the piano choking. It seems that she had a succor in her mouth and some how it got stuck in her throat. David turned and saw what was going on. He went over, picked the little girl up, hit her back, put her in her mother's lap and kept on preaching. The lady took the child back to her seat and they were quiet the rest of the service.

God's message was meant for someone and the devil was not going to take it away. The" devil is like a roaring lion seeking whom he may devour." He does not want God's message to go out and will do whatever it takes to keep it from being preached. What if no one had helped the little girl, she could have died. God allowed the right people to be in the right place. Whether it was to help the little girl or preach the message to the person who needed it!

Our lives are in God's control!

21.

NOTHING IS TO HARD FOR GOD

My father in law, L.J. was a carpenter and he built many churches and tabernacles. He was a very talented man. While working on a little church in Pine Hill, Tennessee ,that he was pastoring, he hurt his leg, but kept working. At that time money was hard to come by and they could not go to a doctor. He let the leg go for several days and then realized that gangrene had set in. His leg was black from his ankle to his knee. His wife, Grace, called all of the church people to the church to come pray for their pastor. When they all arrived they gathered around him and prayed until the glory came down. My husband was watching his dad and looked at his leg. While everyone was praying he watched the normal color return in his dads leg starting with the ankle and going to his knee. His leg was fine! Glory to God! Who takes care of his children.

Isn't it wonderful
what praying can do!

22.

FAITH COMETH BY HEARING

When our second daughter, Cym was about two years old we noticed that she would have a hard time listening to us. We would have to stand almost in front of her for her to understand us. She acted as though she couldn't hear us at all . As she was learning to talk we found that she had problems pronouncing certain letters of the alphabet, like her "F's, "W's, and "S's". The next year it got worse so we took her to a specialist. He tested her hearing and ran numerous test. He wasn't sure exactly what the problem was, but he definitely said she had lost most of her hearing. He suggested that we try putting tubes in her ears. We agreed to try this, We began to pray for God to touch her and bring back her hearing. We went to the hospital a few days later for her to get her tubes put in. It was an in and out type surgery. The doctor said everything went fine. On the way home Cym began to talk and talk and talk. She talked all the way home which was about 20 miles. We laughed at her because we realized this was the first time she probably was hearing her own voice. Now I imagine that you think the tubes did the trick and brought back her ability to hear, well you would be wrong. Within two days those tubes came out, but she still had her hearing. The great physician took control and didn't need the tubes to do it. Over a period of time her pronunciation of words improved because she could hear the sounds. Thank God! He gave our daughter her hearing back.

23.

FAITH OF A CHILD

The first 13 years of my teaching career I taught sixth graders. I truly enjoyed teaching them. They are just at the age to question everything. Every morning in my classroom I would always have devotions. Along with the devotions I would always tell a story to go along with it. Then we would take prayer requests and pray over them. One little girl named Jessica was in my classroom that year. She raised her hand and told how sick her dad was and that they had found cancer in his back. She was so heartbroken when she gave the request. She said that the next week the doctors were going to do surgery to get the cancer out and hopefully save his life.

All 30 students and I gathered round and prayed for Jessica's dad. We prayed that God would take the cancer out and heal him. We prayed that prayer every day until the day of the surgery. Jessica's mother sent her to school that day because she felt it would be better than her sitting in the hospital waiting for news. That morning we did a special prayer for Jessica and her father.

The surgery was to begin around noon. The office had said as soon as they had word from the hospital they would let us know. It was about 12:30 p.m. when someone from the office called for Jessica. I was a little worried because that would have only been 30 minutes into the surgery. I knew it would take longer than that. About 15 minutes later the secretary and Jessica came back. Both of them had big smiles on their faces. The secretary told us that when they went in to do the surgery they could not find any sign of it. He was cancer free. God works in mysterious ways, sometimes he has to show the unbelievers his work.

The next day during devotion we had a lot to talk about. I know this was a great lesson for those students on how prayer works and how to have the faith; But that was not the end. A few years later

Jessica's dad was called into the ministry. God is so Good!

24.

DREAMS

Through the many years I have served the Lord, I have learned that His message can be delivered in many ways; by visions, through His word, through messages from other people and through dreams. Not all dreams are messages, but there are some times that God does talk to us through dreams.

I experienced this when I had gall bladder surgery in Montgomery, Alabama . I was under anesthesia during the surgery, during that time I had a dream about being in heaven. An older gentleman from our church, who had died a couple of weeks earlier, met me. He was so excited to show me something. He kept saying hurry come see what I made. He led me to a place and showed me a beautiful table he had built. This table had intricate carvings in it. As I was looking at it, he said we have to hurry. Then I woke up from the surgery.

This dream bothered me. I kept having the dream over and over. I talked to my husband and asked him if he thought I should share the dream with this man's wife. Someone else had had a vision of her husband and told her. I did not want her to think I was copying him. So I waited, but this dream kept haunting me. Finally I said to myself, "I'm going to tell her the dream and then she can take it or forget about it. Then maybe I won't be worried anymore."

A few days later after church I asked her if I could talk to her. I told her I had had a dream about her husband that I wanted to share with her. I said I don't know what it means, but I hope that it will give you some peace. After I told her about the dream, she stared at me. I asked her if she was alright. She said yes, then she told me that a couple of days before her husband had died he had ordered special tools to make a table like I described. The tools arrived the day after the funeral. After I talked to her I felt like I had done the right thing. I felt like God was telling her that her husband was happy and doing something that he loved.

After telling her the dream, I didn't have that pressure feeling anymore. The dream left my head. I became a vessel for God to use. He used me to send a message of peace to her.

God is always with us. His message could come in all kinds of ways; but he never forgets His children. When we are depressed He sends comfort, when we are lonely He sends people to help in our loneliness, and when we needed salvation He sent His son. God loves you!

25.

HEALING PRAISES

When we came back from Germany we became involved with the ministry of a local church; but God was dealing with us about getting back into Pastoral work. We had been praying for a few months for the Lord to show us what he wanted us to do. One Sunday morning God was moving mightily in our Praise and Worship. We were standing up singing when I looked over and saw David with his hand over his heart and he looked as if he was in great pain. I asked him what was wrong and he said his chest hurt. I asked him if we needed to leave and go to the emergency room. He said no it would be all right. He kept praising God and I could see the pain on his face. Later he told me that at first the more he praised God the harder the pain became, but he said he was determined to continue praising God no matter how bad the pain got. As he kept praising the Lord the pain eased off until it finally stopped. David told me that if he was going to die, he would do so praising God. The pain stopped and we continued Praising God.

About five years later David had another heart attack. This time we got him to a hospital. While the doctors were examining him they found out that he had already had a severe heart attack. He remembered when it happened as if it was that day. David knew that he had had a heart attack during Praise and Worship. We believe that God honored David's praise and took care of his heart attack. He believes that if he had stopped praising God he would have died; but God heard his praise and blessed him by healing him.

And with that touch that day we decided to go back into pastoral work. God takes care of His children and honors them as they praise Him!

26.

RAINBOW PROMISE

In April of 2018, I took a CT scan to check my kidney functions and found myself in a state of shock. The scan showed that I had a 13 cm mass on top of my intestines. About the size of a grapefruit and it was laying on my spinal chord making it hard for me to walk or stand for a long time. Not only did they find the mass, but I also had a small tumor on my adrenal glands and my left kidney. When it rains it pours. The surgeon wanted to get the mass out the next week because it seemed to be growing. We had already planned a cruise vacation before we found out about all of these things. After talking with the doctor she said to go ahead with our plans. She said we needed the rest before we started what was ahead of us.

We went on our cruise and had initially decided not to get off at any ports. Just stay on board and rest, but one of our grandsons had decided he wanted a sharks tooth necklace as a souvenir . So we decided we would get off at Freeport in the Bahamas to find that necklace. My husband went and got me a wheel chair from the ship to use to go on shore because I could not walk the distance.

We went to the triangular market where the tents were set up with their trinkets to sell. We went past the first six tents and as we passed each one they had a purse or hat to try to sell us, but we kept moving along until we got to the last tent. An older lady walked out and handed me a necklace and said, "You need these healing metals". She started telling me her story. When she was 32 she had a grapefruit size tumor in her stomach. She said God supplied a way for her to go to the United States to have it removed. She said God was with her and took care of her. She then looked at me and said, " God is going to take care of you. God is Good." I looked at her and said that I was going to have surgery the next week because I also have a tumor about the size of a grapefruit, but that it was on my intestines. She said that her pastor had given her the scripture in Psalms 37: 1-7 which says for us to

"Fret not,… trust in the Lord, ….Delight thyself in the Lord, …Commit thy ways unto the Lord, ..and then REST". She looked at me and smiled as if she already knew everything, hugged my neck and said that she and her church would be praying for me.

Now some people may say this was a coincidence, but I don't believe in coincidences. I believe that God showed me that no matter where I go he has children that obey him and He will use them to uplift other people. God is in control and I needed that little extra boost from God to remind me that he is there watching over me.

Now I did buy that necklace, not because I thought it had any healing powers, but because when I put it on the metals turned the color of the rainbow. I said this necklace represents my "rainbow promise" from God. I wear it and when people take notice of it I begin to TESTIFY about what the Lord can do! Once I've told the story about the "rainbow promise" I ask them to share it with someone else. I hope people will keep sharing the story and that it will uplift other people.

The story is not over yet. When I came back a contrast MRI was taken to give the doctor a better view of the mass on my intestines, but while he was looking at the mass the doctor found another tumor on my kidney. This tumor had a 85-90% chance of being cancerous. He said when the MRI dye went over the tumor it glistened, which was a sign to him that it was cancerous. So now I'm waiting on the doctors to get together for my surgery. No matter what is thrown at me I stand on God's word that He will take care of me.

The operation was scheduled for May 25th. My doctors didn't think there would be any problems, but boy were they wrong! The first surgeon didn't have any problems removing the tumor which turned out to be larger than a grapefruit. The real problem came when the urologist went to take the cancer off of my kidneys. The top of my kidneys was a stage I cancer which was not seen on the scans, The bottom of my kidney was a stage 4 cancer. By looking at the pictures you would think the cancer was just on the outside of the kidney, but when he went in he found out the cancer had imbedded itself inside the kidney. When he went to remove the kidney I started hemorrhaging and it wouldn't stop. I ended up receiving 5 pints of blood. The operation lasted six hours and my blood pressure dropped to 60/45 and they couldn't make it go up. The nurse asked my family to come into the room to see me because they thought I was not going to make it. My husband left the room and went to call my mother. He told her to start praying because we could be losing Gloria. After calling her my husband had a conversation with God. No sooner had he finished than the nurse came running out telling him that my blood pressure was now normal. She said she didn't know how it happened, But we did.

The next day I had doctors in and out all day. They were doctors who had heard what happened in the operating room and they wanted to meet me. I became the attraction for the day. Nurses came in and said they were so happy to see me because they thought I wasn't going to make it. On Saturday the physical therapist came to get me out of bed to walk some. She said, "I know you probably can't walk far this first time but lets just try it." Not only did I walk down the hallway, I also walked around the nurses station. Again the therapist was amazed that I could do that. I really looked funny walking down the hallway with two full IV poles and a nurse carrying a drainage pouch. By Sunday the nurses started taking out some of the IVs and by Monday drainage tubes were gone. Hour by Hour I became stronger. By Tuesday the doctor asked if I would like to go home. Of course, I said yes! So by Wednesday morning I was on my way home. It's only by the Grace of God that I am alive today. When the doctors couldn't do anything to get my blood pressure up, God came into the picture and took over. I am so thankful for his healing power.

As of this week it has been 6 months since my surgery. I am getting better day by day. My kidney function has gone from 14 to 17. I still have good days and bad days, but God is helping me so my bad days are getting fewer and fewer. I also have been talking to people about my miracle. I see people in the elevator and I begin telling them about what happened to me. I talk to nurses, doctors and anyone else I can get to. I have to tell people what the Lord has done for me.

I have to testify!

CONCLUSION

This is not the end of my stories. Every day God does something special to me or my family. God is so good!

The second book of "Somebody Ought to Testify" will be stories of other people who have experienced something from God and want to share it.

If God has done something for you then you have to Testify!

CONTACT PAGE

If you would like to get in contact with Mrs. Fowler for an event or if you have a story that you would like to share contact her by mail ; 114 Farrell St. Monks Corner, SC. 29461. Please submit stories typed.

Made in the USA
Middletown, DE
26 August 2024

59268751R00055